Let Freedom Ring

The Boston Massacre

By Dee Ready

Consultant:
Susan Goganian
Site Director
The Bostonian Society/Old State House
Boston, Massachusetts

Bridgestone Books
an imprint of Capstone Press
Mankato, Minnesota

Bridgestone Books are published by Capstone Press
151 Good Counsel Drive • P.O. Box 669 • Mankato, Minnesota 56002
http://www.capstone-press.com

Printed in the United States of America

Library of Congress Cataloging-in-Publication Data
Ready, Dee.
      The Boston Massacre / by Dee Ready.
          p. cm. — (Let freedom ring)
      Includes bibliographical references and index.
      Summary: Discusses the situations and events that led to the Boston Massacre, the
      precursor to the American Revolutionary War, including information on the colonies'
      relationship with Britain and the effects of the French and Indian War.
      ISBN 0-7368-1092-7
      1. Boston Massacre, 1770—Juvenile literature. [1. Boston Massacre, 1770.] I. Title.
      II. Series.
      E215.4 .R43 2002
      973.3′113—dc21   2001003427

Editorial Credits
Rebecca Aldridge, editor; Kia Bielke, cover designer, interior layout designer, and interior
illustrator; Jennifer Schonborn, cover production designer; Deirdre Barton, photo researcher

Photo Credits
The Granger Collection, New York (cover); Stock Montage, Inc., 5, 23, 30–31, 32, 35 (large),
39; Rischgitz/Hulton/Archive Photos, 7; Gary Carter/Visuals Unlimited, 11;
MPI/Hulton/Archive Photos, 12, 42 (top); BETTMANN/CORBIS, 15; Hulton/Archive
Photos, 17; North Wind Picture Archives, 19, 20 (both), 25, 27, 33, 37, 42 (bottom); Jeff
Greenberg/Visuals Unlimited, 29; Library of Congress, 35 (small), 43; Kevin
Fleming/CORBIS, 41

1   2   3   4   5   6   07   06   05   04   03   02

Table of Contents

Chapter One

Colonists and the Mother Country

Imagine yourself pitching back and forth on a ship bound for Boston, Massachusetts, in 1754. A few weeks ago, you stepped onto the ship in Britain and waved good-bye. For you, it was an old country packed full of old ideas and ways. You wanted a new life.

After six weeks, you dock in the busy port of Boston. The colonists in this city surprise you. They believe that they can make life better for themselves in the British colonies. These colonists all think for themselves. Within 16 years, on March 5, 1770, the colonists' independent thinking would lead to the Boston Massacre.

For you, as for all the colonists, Britain was the mother country. The 13 colonies were her children whom she would protect. But Britain also would use the 13 colonies to make money.

Many people who came to America from Britain stayed in the port city of Boston, Massachusetts.

Problems with British Laws

In 1651, Parliament, Britain's ruling body, had passed the Navigation Acts. These laws stated that the colonists had to send many of their products to Britain. These goods included furs, sugar, tobacco, rice, and indigo used to make blue dye.

People in Holland or Germany might offer to pay more for these goods, but that did not matter. The law said you and the other colonists must sell to Britain first. You had to buy almost all needed items from Britain, as well.

In Boston, people ignored these laws and got around them by smuggling. In the dark of night, Bostonians unloaded cheaper goods from other countries. They loaded their own goods onto ships. These ships sailed to countries that would pay a higher price for the colonists' goods.

Parliament knew that colonists were breaking trade laws but did nothing about it. Britain was too busy fighting wars in Europe to enforce the trade laws.

The Colonists Are British, Not American

For almost 150 years, the British colonists thought of themselves as British men and women. They followed British laws even though they lived about 3,000 miles (4,800 kilometers) from home.

In Boston, some colonists smuggled goods to avoid Britain's Navigation Acts, which limited trade in the colonies.

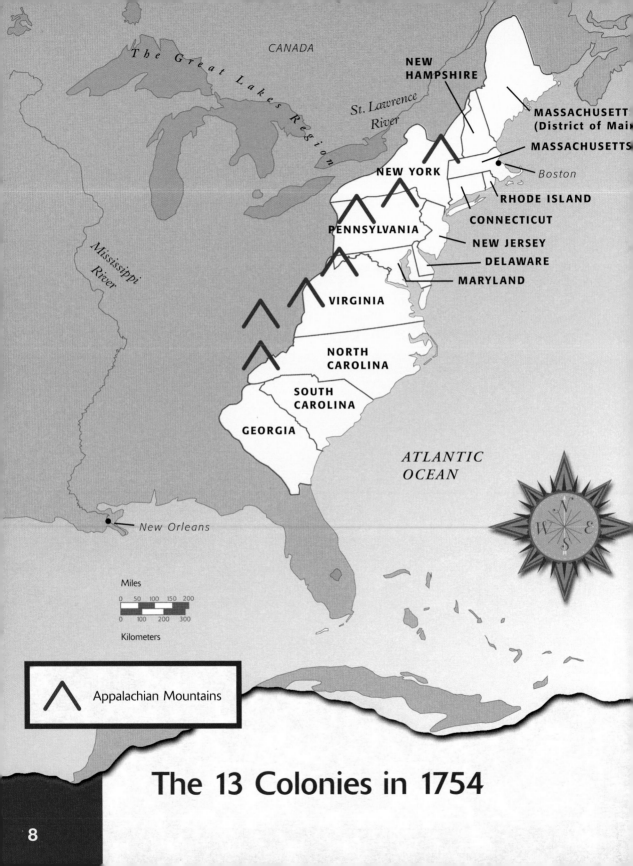

CANADA

The Great Lakes Region

St. Lawrence River

NEW HAMPSHIRE

MASSACHUSETT (District of Main

MASSACHUSETTS

Boston

NEW YORK

RHODE ISLAND

CONNECTICUT

PENNSYLVANIA

NEW JERSEY

DELAWARE

MARYLAND

Mississippi River

VIRGINIA

NORTH CAROLINA

SOUTH CAROLINA

GEORGIA

ATLANTIC OCEAN

New Orleans

Miles

0 50 100 150 200

0 100 200 300

Kilometers

∧ Appalachian Mountains

The 13 Colonies in 1754

8

How Many People Lived in the Colonies?

By 1760, the 13 colonies had a population of more than 1.5 million people. About 500,000 of these people were African slaves.

Some colonists had come from other European countries, such as Scotland, Ireland, Germany, Sweden, and Holland. These colonists also accepted British rule. Colonists did not call themselves Americans. They were simply Europeans far from home.

By 1754, 13 colonies crowded along the Atlantic Coast. Their borders touched, but only British rule kept them together. Most colonists were proud to belong to the mother country.

The French and Indian War (1754–1763) then exploded in America. Things would never again be the same for the colonists.

Chapter Two

A War Brings Change

Both British and French colonists settled in the New World of America. Britain claimed the land that lay along the Atlantic Ocean. France claimed the land along the St. Lawrence River and the Great Lakes. The French trapped fur along the Mississippi River from Canada to New Orleans. Both countries claimed the land between the Appalachian Mountains and the Mississippi River.

The Need for New Land

By 1754, many British colonists felt a hunger to move westward. Colonial farming had used up much of the land near the Atlantic Ocean. Colonists wanted to cross the Appalachian Mountains and find new land to settle and farm in the wilderness.

France did not want British colonists to move westward. French trappers feared that the British would cut down the forests and plant crops on the land. Then the beaver, the main catch for fur trappers, would disappear, and the

British colonists wanted to settle the land west of the Appalachian Mountains (shown here).

French would have nothing to trap and sell. Both Britain and France struggled for control of the land west of the Appalachian Mountains.

The French and Indian War

In 1754, France and Britain began to fight one another in North America. In America, this battle became known as the French and Indian War. Both

Differences over land rights led Britain and its American colonies to battle France in the French and Indian War.

Many American Indians fought alongside the French during the French and Indian War. American Indians thought that the British would try to push them off more land. However, the powerful Iroquois, made up of six American Indian nations, sometimes fought alongside the British.

France and Britain experienced wins and losses during this war. But finally, in 1763, the war came to an end with Britain as the victor.

After the war, France signed a treaty with Britain. This agreement said that France had to give Britain all its land in Canada. France also gave up rights to the land between the Appalachians and the Mississippi River. Britain now claimed most of the land east of the Mississippi.

Beyond the Appalachians

The colonists were excited. The land west of the Appalachians lay before them. The colonists were eager to settle beyond the mountains, but they did not think about the American Indians. These native people had lived in the mountains and forests for

Colonial Militias

Each of the 13 colonies had its own militia. This group of fighting men and teenage boys volunteered to fight in times of emergency. Each militiaman provided his own musket, a type of gun. Several times a year, the militia got together to practice their skills.

The colonial commander of each militia could call his men to military duty at any time. When the men were not training, they farmed their fields and did their regular work.

thousands of years. They did not believe that anyone truly owned the land. The land was for all. British settlers did not agree.

Soon American Indians rose against the British. The warriors fought to protect the land from colonists who had settled on the western frontier.

Britain Tells the Colonists Where to Settle

Britain took notice of the trouble between the colonists and the American Indians. Wars cost money, and Britain was in debt. Britain felt it had to keep settlers from fighting American Indians.

The new British king, George III, issued the Proclamation of 1763. This announcement said that the land west of the Appalachians belonged to the American Indians. No one else could settle there. Colonists already settled in the West were asked to move back to the East.

The proclamation made the colonists angry. Their attitudes about the mother country began to change. "What right does Britain have to keep us off the land?" they asked. Many answered, "No right! None at all!"

Britain's King George III moved to keep tighter control in the colonies after the French and Indian War.

Chapter Three

New Laws Bring Protest

The French and Indian War left Britain with a debt of 133 million pounds ($30 billion today). Parliament needed to pay the debt. King George III felt that the colonists should help. After all, Britain had protected the colonists during the war. The debt belonged to them, too.

King George III and Parliament also believed they had let the colonists have their own way too long. For many years, the colonists had paid no attention to the Navigation Acts. Things had to change, and change they did!

The Sugar Act

In 1764, Parliament passed the Sugar Act to raise money. It enforced taxes on molasses that entered the colonies from non-British ports.

The tax on molasses made the colonists angry because molasses was used to make rum. Most everyone in the colonies and in Britain

The British knew that some colonists would try to avoid the Sugar Act. So Parliament (shown here) offered British customs officers rewards for catching smugglers.

The Daughters of Liberty

Women banded together and formed the Daughters of Liberty. They refused to buy anything made in Britain. They gathered together to spin yarn and weave their own cloth. The colonists had worn clothes made of British materials. Now, they began to wear cloth woven in the colonies. They called this cloth "homespun."

drank rum. The colonists said the tax would keep them from making money when they sold the drink. They protested loudly, and Britain paid attention. In 1766, Parliament lowered the tax. Still, many colonists believed that Parliament had no right to tax them at all.

The Quartering Act

In 1765, Parliament passed the Quartering Act. Britain planned to send between 6,000 and 10,000 soldiers to North America. These soldiers would protect the colonies from American Indians west of the Allegheny Mountains, part of the Appalachian range. The Quartering Act ordered the colonists to supply the soldiers with quarters, or places to live. The colonists also had to pay for the soldiers' food.

Once again, the colonists became angry. They did as little as possible for the soldiers. Of course, the lack of hospitality angered the soldiers. They were far from home, and no one welcomed them. Colonists began making fun of the soldiers. Then soldiers made fun of them, and fights broke out.

On Taxation

Samuel Adams was a leader of the Boston colonists who protested taxation. He said, "If our trade be taxed, why not our lands . . . in short, everything we possess? They tax us without having legal representation."

The Stamp Act

Parliament passed another law in 1765. The Stamp Act put a tax on every piece of printed paper in the 13 colonies. Each piece of paper had to have a

The table on the right lists stamp tax prices for particular pieces of printed paper. Above is an example of a British stamp.

STAMP·OFFICE,
Lincoln's-Inn, 1765.

A

T A B L E

Of the Prices of Parchment and Paper for the Service of *America.*

Parchment.

Skins 18 Inch. by 13, at Fourpence
22 —— by 16, at Six-pence
26 —— by 20, at Eight-pence } each.
28 —— by 23, at Ten-pence
31 —— by 26, at Thirteen-pence

Paper.

Horn at Seven-pence
Fools Cap at Nine-pence
D° with printed Notices } at
for Indentures } 1 s.
Folio Post at One Shilling } each Quire.
Demy—— at Two Shillings
Medium at Three Shillings
Royal—— at Four Shillings
Super Royal at Six Shillings

Paper for Printing

News.

Double Crown at 14 s. } each Ream.
Double Demy at 19 s.

Almanacks.

Book—Crown Paper at 10 s. 6 d.
Book——Fools Cap at 6 s. 6 d. } each Ream.
Pocket — Folio Post at 20 s.
Sheet——Demy at 13 s.

New York—A Foreign Country

When John Rutledge went to New York, he wrote to his mother, "It is my first trip to a foreign country." The colony of New York seemed foreign, or strange, to Rutledge. However, Britain, far across the Atlantic Ocean, was familiar. In fact, Rutledge had gone to school in London, Britain's capital.

Rutledge saw himself as a British man and as a South Carolinian. Protesting the Stamp Act made him and many others into Americans.

stamp that colonists paid for. The act led to loud protests in the streets of Boston. "No!" the colonists said. "We will not pay more to read the newspaper or to get a certificate for marriage!"

In protest, John Rutledge of South Carolina traveled to New York City in October 1765. There, Rutledge met with representatives from eight other colonies. The meeting was the first time the colonies met as one group to protest a British law. The meeting lasted from October 7 to October 25, 1765, and was called the Stamp Act Congress.

"No Taxation without Representation!"

The Stamp Act delegates wrote to Britain. They said that Parliament had no right to tax them. The colonists shouted, "No taxation without representation!" because they had no representatives in Parliament, where laws for the 13 colonies were passed.

Colonists stopped buying printed papers with stamps on them. They refused to buy anything that came to North America from Britain.

Soon, workers in Britain began to lose their jobs because of the boycott. British goods simply sat at the dock. The boycott forced Parliament to get rid of the Stamp Act in 1766. Yet, Parliament said it still had the right to tax in any way it chose.

The Townshend Acts

Parliament passed the Townshend Acts in 1767. These laws taxed glass, lead paint, paper, and tea when they arrived in the colonies. Again, colonists protested by banding together and refusing to pay these taxes. Again, they boycotted British goods.

In 1768, Britain sent more soldiers to the colonies to enforce the Townshend Acts. Parliament told these soldiers to protect British workers who collected the taxes. Many of the soldiers landed in Boston, where they tried to keep order. The king thought that British soldiers could control the colonists, but he was wrong.

Colonists in Boston protested the Stamp Act by burning papers that carried the British stamp.

Chapter Four

Anger and Fear Lead to Death

The people of Boston did not like having soldiers living in their city. But Parliament wanted the soldiers to live in Boston homes. The British hoped that the soldiers' presence would keep the colonists from protesting.

Most people in Boston refused to quarter the soldiers. At first, the soldiers had to sleep in tents outdoors. Some slept on the floor of Faneuil Hall, a Boston meetinghouse. The people of Boston did not care about the soldiers' comfort. Finally, the Massachusetts governor had to quarter the soldiers in empty warehouses and stores.

Bostonians made life difficult for the soldiers. They pushed the soldiers and called them names. Feeling unwanted, the soldiers found ways to make the Bostonians dislike them even more. For example, they practiced drills loudly while the people of Boston sat in church on Sunday.

By 1768, Britain had sent enough soldiers to Boston that soon there was almost one for every eight Bostonians.

Colonial Name-Calling

The colonists called the British soldiers "Redcoats" because of their bright red uniforms. On the night of the Boston Massacre, the colonists insulted the soldiers by calling them "bloody-backs" and "lobsters." Soldiers did not like being called "bloody-backs." The term referred to the whippings soldiers sometimes received across their backs. Colonists called the soldiers "lobsters" because this sea creature turns red when boiled.

The Anger Grows

The soldiers took jobs away from the colonists, which also made Bostonians mad. Britain did not pay soldiers much money, so many soldiers wanted to work at other jobs when they were off duty. The soldiers offered to work for less money than Boston workers did.

Daily, the soldiers and the colonists grew angrier with one another. Finally, Britain moved many of the soldiers out of Boston, but between 400 and 700 soldiers stayed. Even this small number made Bostonians angry.

A Young Barber Insults a Captain

Snow fell all day on March 5, 1770. By that cold Monday evening, more than a foot of snow covered the town. British soldier Hugh White stood guard by one of the government buildings, the Customs House. White had a musket but no bullet in the gun. A young barber named Edward Garrick stopped before the soldier. Garrick claimed that a British officer did not pay his bills.

A young barber making fun of a British officer began what became the Boston Massacre.

White felt that Garrick had insulted the officer by making the rude comment. To get back at Garrick, White swung his musket and hit the young barber under his ear. Garrick ran down the street, calling for help. Soon a crowd of 10 to 12 young boys and men had gathered around White. They shouted, pushed forward, and called him names.

Help Comes to White

Frightened, White ran up the steps of the Customs House behind him. He pounded on the door. Needing help, White shouted, "Turn out the main guard." The soldiers living nearby heard him. Quickly, Captain Thomas Preston and a group of seven soldiers marched into the street. Each soldier fixed a bayonet, or knife, to the end of his musket. However, the eight soldiers did not load their guns.

Suddenly, a church bell rang. At that time of night, a ringing bell meant fire. In a town with wooden buildings, a fire could burn down everything. So people ran from their homes planning to put out a fire. More shouting and pushing people gathered in front of White.

Soon, about 300 or 400 boys and men faced the eight soldiers and their captain. The mob pressed forward. They threw thick pieces of ice and snowballs, hitting the soldiers. They even threw broken clamshells that made up part of the street.

British soldiers fixed bayonets to the ends of their muskets, as shown in this modern-day reenactment.

The British Load Their Guns

The eight soldiers loaded their guns. Some people in the crowd yelled out, "Fire if you dare." Others yelled, "Kill them!" All the colonists thought that British soldiers were not allowed to fire their muskets in peacetime. Colonists believed the soldiers could fire only if someone of the local government told them to. The British army would put on trial a soldier who fired without orders. If found guilty, the soldier could be hanged.

Because of their belief, the colonists did not fear being shot. So they threw more ice and broken clamshells. They hit the soldiers with wooden clubs. Some members of the angry crowd even hit the soldiers' muskets with sticks. These people pressed close to the muzzles, or open ends, of the muskets, daring the soldiers to fire. The soldiers shouted back at the crowd. Noise filled the night.

The First Shot

Captain Preston stood in front of his men. He shouted that the people should go home, that the soldiers were just doing their duty and would not fire without Preston's order.

Just then, a piece of ice hit Private Hugh Montgomery. No one knows for sure what happened next. Did the ice knock Montgomery down? Did pain cause him to step back and slip on

British soldiers faced a mob of angry colonists during the Boston Massacre.

Crispus Attucks

Crispus Attucks went by the name Michael Johnson. Attucks may have been the first man shot during the Boston Massacre.

Historians believe that Attucks was part American Indian, part African American, and part white. It is believed that he was an escaped slave who had spent years at sea as a sailor.

the ice? Whatever happened, when Montgomery got back up, he fired his musket. It may have been an accident. Nothing happened for a moment. Then, filled with panic, the other soldiers fired, too.

Church bells rang out all over Boston. Hundreds of people gathered in the square. There, they saw 11 bodies lying in the snow and frozen mud. Of these, three—Crispus Attucks, Samuel Gray, and James Caldwell—were dead. A few hours later, Samuel Maverick died. Patrick Carr died nine days later. The other six wounded men lived.

Something even more terrible could have happened. The riot could have turned into a battle. However, Massachusetts Governor Thomas Hutchinson pushed through the crowd, demanding calm. Colonel William Dalrymple, who commanded all the soldiers in Boston, joined Hutchinson. After the governor talked the crowd into silence, the British soldiers were led away. Captain Preston was jailed later that night.

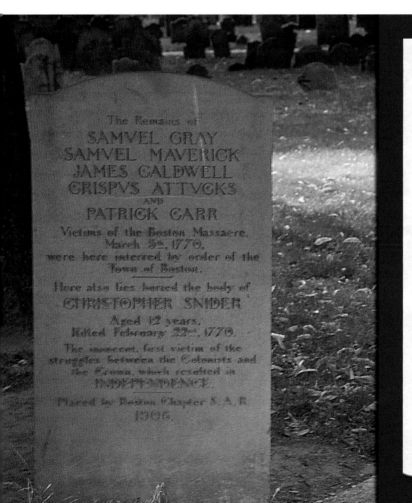

The Funeral

On March 8, 1770, the people of Boston buried four of the men killed in the Boston Massacre. A fifth man, Patrick Carr, died a few days later.

According to people at the scene, between 10,000 and 12,000 people attended the funeral procession to the graveyard. Pictured at left is the victims' gravestone.

Chapter Five

A Riot Becomes a Massacre

The murder trial of Captain Preston began in October 1770. John Adams and Josiah Quincy Jr. were his lawyers. During Preston's trial, witnesses gave different stories about what had happened on the night of March 5, 1770. Several said that Captain Preston never shouted, "Fire!"

Other witnesses remembered Preston saying, "Not to fire!" They thought that the noise of the crowd drowned out all but the last of his words. After all the witnesses spoke, the jury found Preston not guilty.

The Trial of the Soldiers

Adams and Quincy also defended the eight soldiers in their November trial. Once again, stories differed. Many witnesses remembered no rocks or ice, no shouting or pushing. Others admitted that the crowd had become a mob. They said the soldiers had fired because they feared for their lives.

THE

TRIAL

OF

William Wemms, James Hartegan, William M'Cauley, Hugh White, Matthew Killroy, William Warren, John Carrol, and Hugh Montgomery,

Soldiers in his Majesty's 29th Regiment of Foot,

FOR THE MURDER OF

Crispus Attucks, Samuel Gray, Samuel Maverick, James Caldwell, and Patrick Carr,

On MONDAY-EVENING, the 5th of MARCH, 1770,

AT THE

Superior Court of Judicature, Court of Assize, and general Goal Delivery, held at BOSTON.

The 27th Day of November, 1770, by Adjournment.

BEFORE

The Hon. BENJAMIN LYNDE, JOHN CUSHING, PETER OLIVER, and EDMUND TROWBRIDGE, ESQUIRES, JUSTICES of said COURT.

Published by Permission of the COURT.

Taken in SHORT-HAND by JOHN HODGSON.

BOSTON:

Printed by J. FLEMING, and sold at his PRINTING-OFFICE, nearly opposite the White-Horse Tavern in Newbury-Street.

M,DCC,LXX.

John Adams (pictured here) was Samuel Adams's cousin. John thought that the colonial men who had started the riot against White were troublemakers.

One Who Did Not Blame the Soldiers

Patrick Carr died nine days after being shot in the Boston Massacre. Dr. John Jeffries took care of him. Jeffries asked Carr if he thought the British soldiers would fire at the crowd. Later, as a witness at the trial, Jeffries said:

"He [Carr] told me he thought the soldiers would have fired long before. I asked him whether he thought the soldiers were abused [hurt] a great deal, after they went down there. He said, he thought they were. I asked him whether he thought the soldiers would have been hurt, if they had not fired. He said he really thought they would, for he heard many voices cry out, kill them. I asked him then, meaning to close all, whether he thought they fired in self-defense, or on purpose to destroy the people. He said he really thought they did fire to defend themselves; that he did not blame the man whoever he was, that shot him."

The jury found six soldiers not guilty. It found the other two soldiers guilty of killing without meaning to do so. One of the two was Hugh Montgomery, who may have fired the first shot. The two men were branded on their thumbs. This painful marking with a hot iron was a common punishment of the time.

The Making of a Massacre

A massacre means the cruel killing of many helpless people. What happened on March 5, 1770, in Boston was not a massacre. However, Samuel Adams, Paul Revere, and others used the event to keep the colonists angry with Britain.

After the Boston Massacre, Samuel Adams (at left, pointing finger) warned the British that they could count on more trouble if things did not change.

Playing Fair

Josiah Quincy Jr. was the only lawyer in town who said he would help the soldiers. He had one condition: John Adams had to defend them, too. Adams agreed to become the soldiers' lawyer when he found this out.

Many Bostonians could not understand how John Adams and Josiah Quincy Jr. could represent the British soldiers. However, Adams believed that everyone deserved a fair trial.

Samuel Adams wanted the colonists to rise up against the British. He quickly named the event of March 5, 1770, a "horrible massacre." He called the men who died "martyrs." He said these men had freely given their lives for what they believed. Samuel Adams called the British soldiers "bloody butchers."

Paul Revere, a Bostonian who worked with silver, created a picture to help the colonists remember the "Boston Massacre." Many things in the picture did not really happen. However, Massachusetts and the other colonies printed this picture and passed it around as truth.

Revere's Propaganda

Propaganda is information that people use to influence how other people think. Some of the information may be false. Paul Revere's picture of the Boston Massacre became an important piece of propaganda in the colonies.

Revere drew some things that really did not happen. For example, he uses light blue for the sky as if the event happened during the day instead of at night. Captain Preston's arm is raised to order the soldiers to fire, which never happened. Revere also labeled the Customs House "Butcher's Hall." Most importantly, Revere showed peaceful Bostonians, not an angry mob.

Monument for the Massacre

In 1888, Massachusetts put up a monument to the five men who died in the Boston Massacre. In one corner are the words of Daniel Webster, a famous lawyer from the early days of the United States. He said, "From that moment we may date the severance [cutting apart] of the British Empire." Webster thought that the event on March 5, 1770, began to cut the colonies from Britain.

In another corner, the words of John Adams are carved: "On that night the foundation of American Independence was laid."

Things Settle Down—for a While

After March 5, 1770, life quieted down in Boston. The British soldiers went to Castle William, a fort on an island in Boston Harbor. Parliament had put an end to the Townshend Acts the same day the Boston Massacre happened. Britain kept only the tax on tea.

Seeing Britain's actions, the colonists stopped boycotting British goods. However, they still refused to drink tea shipped from Britain.

Parliament thought trouble in the colonies was finished. But in 1773, trouble arose in Boston again. The Boston Tea Party occurred as a protest against Britain's policies on tea. Tension between Britain and the colonies was renewed and led to revolution.

The Boston Massacre had helped the colonists begin to think of themselves as Americans. The event was an important stepping-stone to the American Revolution (1775–1783).

The cobblestone circle at the bottom of this photo lies in front of the Old State House. (The Customs House no longer exists.) It marks the spot where the Boston Massacre took place.

TIMELINE

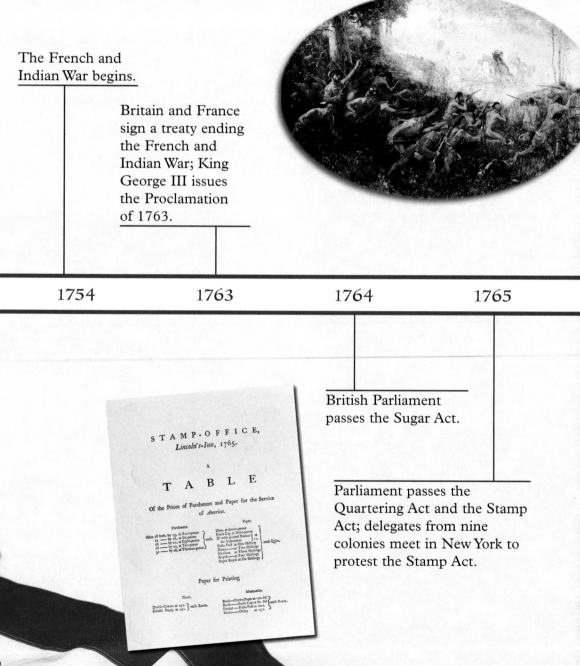

The French and Indian War begins.

Britain and France sign a treaty ending the French and Indian War; King George III issues the Proclamation of 1763.

| 1754 | 1763 | 1764 | 1765 |

British Parliament passes the Sugar Act.

STAMP·OFFICE,
Lincoln's-Inn, 1765.

A

T A B L E

Of the Prices of Parchment and Paper for the Service of *America.*

Paper for Printing

Parliament passes the Quartering Act and the Stamp Act; delegates from nine colonies meet in New York to protest the Stamp Act.

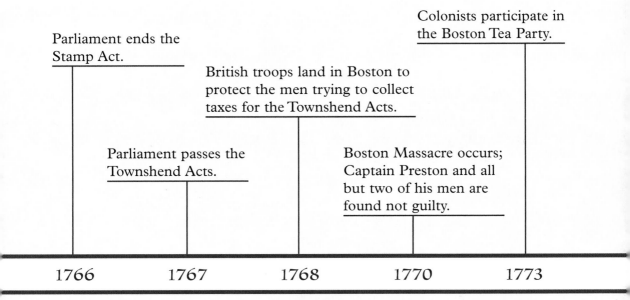

Parliament ends the
Stamp Act.

Colonists participate in
the Boston Tea Party.

British troops land in Boston to
protect the men trying to collect
taxes for the Townshend Acts.

Parliament passes the
Townshend Acts.

Boston Massacre occurs;
Captain Preston and all
but two of his men are
found not guilty.

1766   1767   1768   1770   1773

Glossary

boycott (BOI-kot)—to refuse to buy certain goods as a means of protest

delegate (DEL-uh-guht)—a person chosen to represent other people at a meeting

foreign (FOR-uhn)—strange; coming from another country.

massacre (MASS-uh-kur)—the cruel killing of many people

militia (muh-LISH-uh)—a group of people trained to fight but who serve only in times of emergency

Parliament (PAR-luh-muhnt)—Britain's governing body of lawmakers

propaganda (prop-uh-GAN-duh)—information that people use to influence how other people think

protest (PROH-test)—a demonstration against something

representation (rep-ri-zen-TAY-shuhn)—an elected body that acts for others in government

revolution (rev-uh-LOO-shuhn)—an uprising that attempts to change a way of government

smuggle (SMUHG-uhl)—to bring goods illegally into a country

taxation (taks-AY-shuhn)—a requirement that people and businesses pay money to support a government

For Further Reading

Gourley, Catherine. *Welcome to Felicity's World: 1774.* The American Girls Collection. Middleton, Wisc.: Pleasant Company Publications, 1999.

Hakim, Joy. *From Colonies to Country.* History of US. New York: Oxford University Press, 1999.

Lukes, Bonnie L. *The Boston Massacre.* Famous Trials. San Diego, Calif.: Lucent, 1998.

Miller, Susan Martins. *The Boston Massacre.* American Adventure. Uhrichsville, Ohio: Barbour & Co., 1997.

Places of Interest

Boston Massacre Monument
On the Boston Common
bordered by Boylston, Arlington,
Charles, Beacon, Park, and
Tremont Streets
Boston, Massachusetts
The statue dedicated to the men
who died in the Boston Massacre

Boston Massacre Site
In front of the Old State House at
Devonshire and State Streets
Boston, Massachusetts
This circle of cobblestones marks
the actual site where the shooting
took place.

Old Granary Burying Ground
Intersection of Park and
Tremont Streets
Boston, Massachusetts
The five colonists who died in the
Boston Massacre are buried here;
you also can see the graves of
Samuel Adams and Paul Revere.

Old State House
206 Washington Street
Boston, MA 02109-1713
Has a permanent exhibit about
the Boston Massacre and the
events surrounding it

The Paul Revere House
19 North Square
Boston, MA 02113
Home of the man who made the
most memorable image of the
Boston Massacre

Internet Sites

Africans in America Part 2: Crispus Attucks
http://www.pbs.org/wgbh/aia/part2/2p24.html
Gives information about Crispus Attucks and his part in the
Boston Massacre

The History Place: American Revolution
http://www.historyplace.com/unitedstates/revolution
Provides links to timelines of American Revolution events

Institute for Learning Technologies: Columbia University
http://www.ilt.columbia.edu/k12/history/blacks/massacre.html
Provides a written record of what was said at Captain Preston's trial

KidInfo: American Revolution
*http://www.kidinfo.com/american_history/american_revolution.
html*
Offers links related to the American Revolution and its many events

Kidport Reference Library: Social Studies—Boston Massacre
*http://www.kidport.com/reflib/usahistory/americanrevolution/
bostonmassacre.htm*
Has links to information on the Boston Massacre and the
American Revolution

Index